The author and publisher gratefully acknowledge the following permissions granted to reprint copyrighted material:

"December" is reprinted by permission of the author, Aileen Fisher, who controls rights. From *That's Why*, Nelson & Sons, copyright 1946 by Aileen Fisher. Copyright renewed.

"little tree" is reprinted from *Tulips & Chimneys* by E. E. Cummings, edited by George James Firmage, by permission of Liveright Publishing Corporation. Copyright 1923, 1925, and renewed 1951, 1953 by E. E. Cummings. Copyright © 1973, 1976 by the Trustees for the E. E. Cummings Trust. Copyright © 1973, 1976 by George James Firmage.

Library of Congress Cataloging-in-Publication Data: Baby's Christmas treasury / [compiled by] Kay Chorao.   p.   cm.   SUMMARY: A collection of poems, stories, and songs about Christmas.   ISBN 0-679-80198-7 (trade)—ISBN 0-679-90198-1 (lib. bdg.)   1. Christmas— Literary collections.   [1. Christmas—Literary collections.]   I. Chorao, Kay.   PZ5.B123   1991   808.8'033—dc20   90-45872

Manufactured in the United States of America   10 9 8 7 6 5 4 3 2 1

Baby's Christmas Treasury

KAY CHORAO

Random House ⌂ New York

December

I like days
with a snow-white collar,
and nights when the moon
is a silver dollar,
and hills are filled
with eiderdown stuffing
and your breath makes smoke
like an engine puffing.

I like days
when feathers are snowing,
and all the eaves
have petticoats showing,
and the air is cold
and the wires are humming,
but you feel all warm…
with Christmas coming.

Aileen Fisher

Deck the Hall

Deck the hall with boughs of holly,
Fa la la la la, la la la la.
'Tis the season to be jolly,
Fa la la la la, la la la la.
Don we now our gay apparel,
Fa la la, fa la la, la la la.
Toll the ancient yuletide carol,
Fa la la la la, la la la la.

See the blazing yule before us,
Fa la la la la, la la la la.
Strike the harp and join the chorus,
Fa la la la la, la la la la.
Follow me in merry measure,
Fa la la, fa la la, la la la.
While I tell of yuletide treasure,
Fa la la la la, la la la la.

Traditional Welsh Carol

A Christmas Alphabet

A is for Angel

B is for Bell

C is for Candle

D is for Drum

E is for Elves

F is for Fireplace

G is for Gingerbread

H is for Holly

I is for Ice Skates

J is for Jack-in-the-box

K is for Kings

L is for Lights

M is for Mistletoe

N is for Nutcracker

O is for Ornaments

P is for Presents

Q is for Quilt

R is for Ribbon

S is for Santa

T is for Tree

U is for Unicorn

V is for Violin

W is for Wreath

X is for Xylophone

Y is for Yule Log

Z is for Zebra

little tree

little tree
little silent Christmas tree
you are so little
you are more like a flower

who found you in the green forest
and were you very sorry to come away?
see   i will comfort you
because you smell so sweetly

i will kiss your cool bark
and hug you safe and tight
just as your mother would,
only don't be afraid

look   the spangles
that sleep all the year in a dark box
dreaming of being taken out and allowed to shine,
the balls the chains red and gold the fluffy threads,

put up your little arms
and i'll give them all to you to hold
every finger shall have its ring
and there won't be a single place dark or unhappy

then when you're quite dressed
you'll stand in the window for everyone to see
and how they'll stare!
oh but you'll be very proud

and my little sister and i will take hands
and looking up at our beautiful tree
we'll dance and sing
"Noel Noel"

e. e. cummings

look   the spangles
that sleep all the year in a dark box
dreaming of being taken out and allowed to shine,
the balls the chains red and gold the fluffy threads,

put up your little arms
and i'll give them all to you to hold
every finger shall have its ring
and there won't be a single place dark or unhappy

then when you're quite dressed
you'll stand in the window for everyone to see
and how they'll stare!
oh but you'll be very proud

and my little sister and i will take hands
and looking up at our beautiful tree
we'll dance and sing
"Noel Noel"

e. e. cummings

Do Not Open Until Christmas

I shake-shake,
Shake-shake,
Shake the package well.

But what there is inside of it,
Shaking will not tell.

James S. Tippett

Christmas Is Coming

Christmas is coming, the geese are getting fat,
Please to put a penny in an old man's hat;
If you haven't got a penny, a ha'penny will do,
If you haven't got a ha'penny, then God bless you.

Traditional English Rhyme

Merry Are the Bells

Merry are the bells, and merry would they ring,
Merry was myself, and merry would I sing,
With a merry ding-dong, happy, gay, and free,
And a merry sing-song, happy let us be!

Anonymous

Christmas Counting in the Forest

All the animals in the forest are busy.
They are getting ready for their Christmas party.

"I'm bringing ten candy canes," growled Bear. 10
"What will you bring, Deer?"

"I will bring nine icicles," said Deer softly. 9
"What will Fox bring?"

"Eight shiny balls!" said Fox. 8
"What about you, Raccoon?"

"Seven sparkling snowflakes!" said Raccoon. 7
"What will you bring, Rabbit?"

"I have six little Santas," sniffed Rabbit. 6
"And you, Squirrel?"

"Here are five silver acorns," said Squirrel. 5
"What about you, Dog?"

"Four bells!" barked Dog. 4
"What will you bring, Cat?"

"I will bring three golden trumpets," purred Cat. 3
"And what have you got, Mouse?"

"Two toy soldiers," squeaked Mouse. 2

Then out of the clear blue sky swooped a bird.
"What do you have for the party, Bird?"

"A star. I will bring one shining star." 1

"We're ready at last," Bear growled. "Now let the
party begin!" So they took their gifts and had a
very special Christmas in the forest. Can you guess
what they did? Turn the page and see!

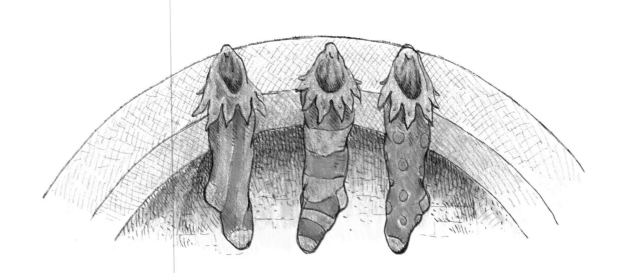

Stocking Song on Christmas Eve

Welcome, Christmas! heel and toe
Here we wait three in a row.
Come, good Santa Claus, we beg—
Fill us tightly, foot and leg.

Fill us quickly, ere you go—
Fill us till we overflow.
That's the way! and leave us more
Heaped in piles upon the floor.

Here we hang till someone nimbly
Jumps with treasure down the chimney.
Bless us! how he'll tickle us!
Funny old St. Nicholas!

Mary Mapes Dodge

The Velveteen Rabbit

Once there was a Velveteen Rabbit.

On Christmas morning he sat in the top of the Boy's stocking with a sprig of holly between his paws, and the Boy loved him! But then all the aunts and uncles came to dinner, and there was a great rustling of tissue paper and unwrapping of parcels, and in the excitement of looking at all the new presents the Rabbit was forgotten.

After that he lived in the nursery with the other toys. They all made fun of the little Rabbit, telling him that *they* were Real and *he* was just a stuffed toy. Only the Skin Horse was kind to him.

"What is Real?" asked the Rabbit.

"When a child loves you until all your hair has been loved off and you are very shabby–then you become Real," said the Skin Horse.

The Rabbit sighed. He longed to become Real.

Then one night the Boy could not find his favorite toy dog, and he took the Rabbit to bed with him instead. Every night after that the Velveteen Rabbit slept in the Boy's bed. The Rabbit was so happy he never noticed how his beautiful velveteen fur was getting shabbier and shabbier, and his tail coming unsewn, and all the pink rubbed off his nose where the Boy had kissed him.

The Boy took the Rabbit everywhere. One day they were playing in the garden when the Rabbit saw two strange beings creep out of the woods.

They were rabbits! But they were furry and new, and they moved all by themselves!

The wild rabbits looked closely at the little Rabbit. "He hasn't got any hind legs!" they said. "He isn't real!"

"But I *am* Real! The Boy said so!" cried the Velveteen Rabbit. Just then there was a sound of footsteps, and the two strange rabbits disappeared into the bushes.

Weeks passed, and the Boy kept on loving the little Rabbit—so hard that he loved all his whiskers off. But the Boy and the Rabbit didn't mind at all because when you are Real shabbiness doesn't matter.

And then one day the Boy fell ill with scarlet fever. He was too ill to play. But the Rabbit stayed with him. He knew the Boy needed him.

At last the Boy got well. But the doctor said, "That old bunny is full of scarlet fever germs. It must be burned at once."

So the little Rabbit was carried out to the end of the garden to be burned. And as he lay there alone, a tear, a real tear, trickled down his shabby velveteen nose and fell to the ground.

Then a wonderful thing happened. A lovely Fairy appeared. She came close to the little Rabbit and gathered him up in her arms and kissed him on his velveteen nose that was all damp from crying.

"Little Rabbit, don't you know who I am?" The Rabbit looked up at her, and it seemed to him that he had seen her face before, but he couldn't think where.

"I am the Christmas Fairy," she said. "I take care of the Christmas toys that children have loved. When they have grown old and shabby from love, I turn them into Real."

And then she kissed him. "Run and play, little Rabbit!"

The little Rabbit sat quite still. Then he saw that he had hind legs, and soft fur, and long whiskers, and ears that twitched by themselves. He was a Real Rabbit at last!

When summer came, the Boy went out to play in the garden and saw two rabbits by the edge of the wood.

"Why, he looks just like my old Bunny," he said.

But he never knew that it really was his own Velveteen Rabbit, come back to look at the child who had first helped him to be Real.

Based on the story by Margery Williams

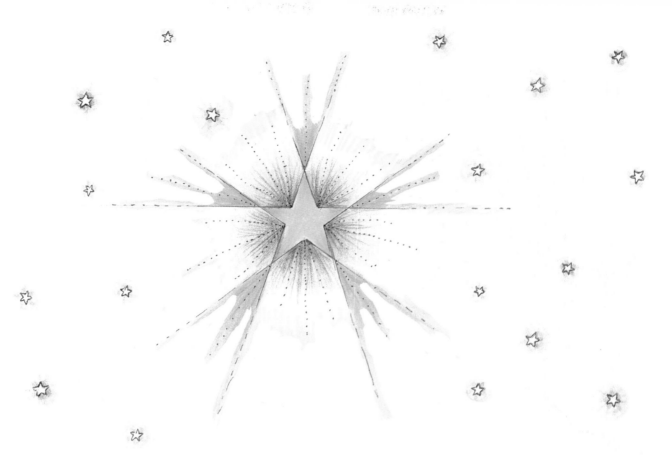

"I," said the dove from the rafters high,
"I cooed him to sleep so he would not cry,
I cooed him to sleep, my mate and I.
I," said the dove from the rafters high.

And every beast, by some good spell,
In the stable dark was glad to tell,
Of the gift he gave Immanuel,
The gift he gave Immanuel.

12th-Century English Carol

Jingle Bells

Dashing through the snow,
In a one-horse open sleigh,
O'er the fields we go,
Laughing all the way;
Bells on bob-tail ring,
Making spirits bright;
What fun it is to ride and sing
A sleighing song tonight!

Jingle bells, jingle bells,
Jingle all the way;
Oh, what fun it is to ride
In a one-horse open sleigh!
Jingle bells, jingle bells,
Jingle all the way;
Oh, what fun it is to ride
In a one-horse open sleigh!

James Pierpont

A Visit from St. Nicholas

'Twas the night before Christmas, when all through the house
Not a creature was stirring, not even a mouse;
The stockings were hung by the chimney with care,
In hopes that St. Nicholas soon would be there.
The children were nestled all snug in their beds,
While visions of sugar-plums danced in their heads;
And mamma in her 'kerchief and I in my cap
Had just settled our brains for a long winter's nap—
When out on the lawn there arose such a clatter,
I sprang from my bed to see what was the matter.
Away to the window I flew like a flash,
Tore open the shutters, and threw up the sash.
The moon on the breast of the new-fallen snow
Gave the luster of midday to objects below;
When what to my wondering eyes should appear,
But a miniature sleigh and eight tiny reindeer,
With a little old driver, so lively and quick,
I knew in a moment it must be St. Nick.

More rapid than eagles his coursers they came,
And he whistled, and shouted, and called them by name:
"Now, Dasher! now, Dancer! now, Prancer and Vixen!
On, Comet! on, Cupid! on, Donder and Blitzen!
To the top of the porch! To the top of the wall!
Now dash away! Dash away! Dash away, all!"
As dry leaves that before the wild hurricane fly,
When they meet with an obstacle, mount to the sky;
So up to the house-top the coursers they flew
With the sleigh full of toys, and St. Nicholas too.

And then, in a twinkling, I heard on the roof
The prancing and pawing of each little hoof–
As I drew in my head, and was turning around,
Down the chimney St. Nicholas came with a bound.
He was dressed all in fur from his head to his foot,
And his clothes were all tarnished with ashes and soot;
A bundle of toys he had flung on his back,
And he looked like a pedlar just opening his pack.
His eyes–how they twinkled; his dimples, how merry!
His cheeks were like roses, his nose like a cherry!
His droll little mouth was drawn up like a bow,
And the beard of his chin was as white as the snow;
The stump of a pipe he held tight in his teeth,
And the smoke it encircled his head like a wreath;
He had a broad face and a little round belly
That shook, when he laughed, like a bowl full of jelly.
He was chubby and plump, a right jolly old elf,
And I laughed when I saw him, in spite of myself;
A wink of his eye and a twist of his head
Soon gave me to know I had nothing to dread;
He spoke not a word but went straight to his work,
And filled all the stockings; then turned with a jerk,
And laying his finger aside of his nose,
And giving a nod, up the chimney he rose;
He sprang to his sleigh, to his team gave a whistle,
And away they all flew like the down of a thistle.
But I heard him exclaim, ere he drove out of sight,
"Happy Christmas to all, and to all a good night!"

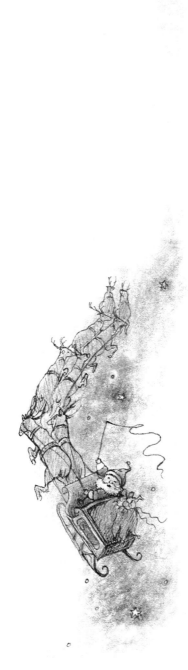

Clement C. Moore

We Wish You a Merry Christmas

We wish you a merry Christmas,
We wish you a merry Christmas,
We wish you a merry Christmas,
And a happy New Year!

Glad tidings we bring
To you and your kin,
We wish you a merry Christmas
And a happy New Year!

Now bring us some figgy pudding,
Now bring us some figgy pudding,
Now bring us some figgy pudding,
And bring some out here!

For we all like our figgy pudding,
We all like our figgy pudding,
We all like our figgy pudding,
So bring some out here.

We won't go until we get some,
We won't go until we get some,
We won't go until we get some,
So bring some out here!

Traditional English Carol

Now Christmas Is Come

Now Christmas is come,
    Let's beat up the drum
And call all our neighbors together,
    And when they appear,
Let's make them such cheer
    As will keep out the wind and the weather!

Washington Irving